THE 200 *funniest* SPORTS STORIES EVER TOLD

Paul King & Greg MacNeil

W9-CCU-531

SEAL BOOKS
McClelland-Bantam, Inc.
Toronto

The 200 Funniest Sports Stories Ever Told

Seal Paperback / November 1995

ISBN 0-770-42720-0

Seal Books are published by McClelland-Bantam, Inc. Its trademark, consisting of
the words "Seal Books" and the portrayal of a seal, is the property of
McClelland-Bantam, Inc., 105 Bond Street, Toronto, Ontario M5B 1Y3, Canada.
This trademark has been duly registered in the Trademark Office of Canada. The
trademark consisting of the words "Bantam Books" and the portrayal of a
rooster is the property of and is used with the consent of Bantam Books, 1540
Broadway, New York, New York 10036. This trademark has been duly registered
in the Trademark Office of Canada and elsewhere.

PRINTED IN U.S.A.
COVER PRINTED IN U.S.A.
UNI - 0 9 8 7 6 5 4 3 2 1

Some of the funniest things happen in team dressing rooms. Whenever I leave a hockey arena, a ballpark, or even a tennis club or a fishing lodge, I always feel better. Usually, it's due to a combination of sport, comraderie, a couple of beers and funny stories.

So we set out to capture that good feeling by publishing a digest of some of the funniest sports stories ever told. I was concerned, at first, that some of the stories involved athletes from earlier generations; but, writer Paul King said "Look Greg, funny is funny... doesn't matter if it was yesterday or fifty years ago." Paul was right. And we quickly expanded from 100 stories to 200.

Our sincere thanks to the many, on our "special teams", who helped develop the concept, who motivated and who did the real work. They include: Gary Alles, The Fan 590, Lilia Lozinski, Mike Miville, Neil Morton, The "Blue" Team, Steve Turton and our illustration and design team of Kathryn Adams, Tracy John and Susan Meingast.

We hope you have as much enjoyment reading these stories as we had in putting them together for you.

> *"When I was a child, I thought as a child.*
> *But when I became a man,*
> *I put away childish things."*
> — Ezekiel

> *"Sports is the toy department of life."*
> — Jimmy Cannon

Well! There it is.

You either grow up, or you don't.

If it came to a choice, we'd scratch old Zeke. Jimmy Cannon had a lot more laughs.

Besides, life's tough enough without ditching childhood.

So let's trip back to Jimmy's toy floor. It's a mad, manic landscape of pea-green outfields, blue lines, square rings, macramed hoops, and sickening sand-traps.

They're turfed, iced, planked, or canvassed combat zones — overrun by zealous sluggers, slicers, slam-dunkers, and oftsozzled scribes.

Still, while most jocks are praised for their athletic prowess, many have also been screamingly funny. Guys like Dean, Berra, and Stengel are already immortalized for their gems of inanity. But there's also a swelling roster of runners-up.

Besides the busted noses, egos, and contracts, there's laughs in them there locker rooms. Because, in Cannon's tumultuous toy department, grown-up athletes will always be boys. Or totally bananas.

Read on. We kid you not.

Flight attendant to Heavyweight boxing champ **Muhammad Ali:**

"Please Mr. Ali, fasten your seat-belt."

"Superman don't need no seat-belt."

"Yeah, and superman don't need no plane either."

Casey **Stengel** was distraught when the Boston Braves made him president, manager, and right-fielder of its farm club at Worcester, Massachusetts. But on the final day of the season, Casey cleverly effected his escape. As manager, he released Stengel the rightfielder. As president, he fired Stengel the manager. And then, as Stengel, he resigned as president.

An elderly Scot played golf every day until his eyesight began to go. His optometrist confirmed there was nothing he could do, but attempted to cheer Angus up. "Listen," he said, "you're still a healthy man, and there's nothing wrong with your game. Just get someone to spot the ball for you."

So Angus asked his old friend Jock, who was 89 but had perfect vision, if he'd caddy for him. Jock said he'd be delighted.

The following morning, the two stood at the tee as Angus swacked a magnificent shot down the fairway. "Did you *see* that?" he blurbed with excitement.

"Aye," said Jock, "like a hawk. All the way."

"Ah, great," said Angus. "Now *where* did it go?"

Jock shook his head. "I don't remember."

A businessman once told Montreal goalie **Jacques Plante** how much he envied him. "Yeah?" sniffed Plante. "Well, how would you like it if you were in your office and made *one* little mistake. And suddenly a bright red light flashed on behind you and 18,000 people screamed, "Get that @#$%* bum outta here!"

During a benefit tournament, the famous blind golfer **Charlie Boswell** was standing near the tee when a player lashed at a ball. Turning to his caddy, Charlie murmured, "Worst swing I ever heard."

In 1959, an old-time major league player was asked, "What would **Ty Cobb** bat today?"

"Oh," pondered the oldster, "maybe .305 or .310."

"What?" spluttered the sportscaster. "Do you *really* think that's *all* Cobb could bat?"

"Well, yeah," sniffed the old-timer. "Ya gotta remember he's 72."

Cobb, the first player elected to baseball's Hall of Fame, raised base-stealing to a science. When a catcher was asked, "What do you do when Cobb breaks for second?" the catcher snorted, "I throw to third."

Entering a hotel room, the chambermaid discovered a guest standing in the bathtub. He was wearing waders, a floppy hat hooked with fishing flies, and a creel slung across his shoulder. As he flicked a dry fly into the water at his feet, he didn't even glance at the maid.

Fleeing straight to the manager's office, she wheezed, "Hey boss, there's a fruitcake up in 1231. If you want me to clean that room, you better get him outta there."

So the manager hustled to the room to find the flake still casting. Deciding to approach the situation slowly, the manager smiled. "Hi there, fella. Catching any fish?"

The guy turned and glowered. "*You crazy?*" he sneered. "In a *bathtub?*"

Lee Trevino loves the story about the executive who got a new set of golf clubs upon his retirement. Never having played before, he walked to the first tee and asked his caddy what he was supposed to do. The caddy pointed down the fairway and said, "You hit the ball towards that flag."

So the executive swung, and his drive was miraculous. The ball landed smack on the green, three inches from the hole. "What do I do next?" he asked.

"You hit the ball into the cup," said the caddy.

The executive snorted. "*Now* you tell me."

Another novice businessman named Plunkett was luckier. His caddy not only pointed out the flag, but described the small hole the ball had to go into. So Plunkett swung. The ball arced high and true, landing on the green. When they got there, the caddy was staggered to see it in the cup.

Plunkett casually picked it up, and said, "What next?" The caddy pointed, speechless, towards the second hole. But this time the ball sliced – before hitting the tree, and caroming back towards the green. And sure enough, when the caddy reached the cup, the ball was in it.

Plunkett retrieved it, stared at the third hole, and swung again. This time, his drive was short, but the ball kept hopping onto the green – stopping an eyelash short of the cup. The caddy gulped in disbelief.

"Well," shrugged Plunkett, "it had to happen. A beginner's a beginner."

Vancouver Canucks' owner **Frank Griffiths** kept insisting that his coach, **Roger Neilson**, should be fired. But each time he did, general manager **Harry Neale** vehemently defended him.

So when Griffiths flew off for a Hawaiian vacation, he made Neale promise to keep him posted on the team's nightly progress. Two nights later, after losing to the Edmonton Oilers, Neale reluctantly phoned Griffiths the news.

"That's *it*!" boomed Griffiths. "Have you fired Neilson yet?"

"But you can't blame *Roger*," said Neale. "Gretzky slammed us tonight like a one-man SWAT squad."

"FIRE him!" snarled Griffiths.

"Hey," said Neale, "we lost a tough one, but the team played *well*."

There was total silence. Thinking his boss was reconsidering, Neale was encouraged.

Then Griffiths was back on the line. "Listen to me, Harry," he purred. "There's no point in having *two* men fired over one decision, is there?"

"You're *right*!" said Harry. "Roger's *gone*!"

One of the most amazing plays in baseball was called by long-time broadcaster **Byrum Saam:** *"There goes a long fly to the left. He's going back...back...his head hits the wall. It bounces off. He reaches down, picks it up, and throws it to second base."*

Sportswriter **John Mooney** was famed for his sage advice. For example, he once advised an entire ball club: "If your doctor tells you to watch your drinking, find a bar with a mirror."

An Irishman was golfing in Scotland when he sliced his ball into a cemetery fenced-in beside the fairway. While searching through the graveyard with his partner, he spotted a tombstone that read:

Sandy McTavish
A Loving Husband
A Kind Father

"Look at this," he snorted. "*Typically* Scotch. Three men in one grave."

Eddie "**The Pistol**" **Dorohoy** was only 19 when he joined the Montreal Canadiens. But even then, his mouth was bigger than he was. In the middle of rushes, he'd suddenly stop and demand a conference to tell superstars **Elmer Lach and Rocket Richard**, "You guys are out of position."

After coach **Dick Irvin** forced Eddie to increase his weight from 150 to 162, Irvin then complained he was "too soft and fat."

"Sounds to me," retorted Eddie, "that you're talking about your head."

He was, of course, instantly benched. But even from there, he kept proffering advice. Finally, coach Irvin snapped. "Dammit, why can't you learn to shut your trap, and sink a puck instead?"

Eddie was obviously not fazed. "Because, from the angle of the bench I'm sitting on," he glowered, "I'm lucky to even touch the puck."

A lot of sport stars hail from tiny towns. And a lot of their descriptions of their hometown burgs are classics. For instance:

Clemson basketball star **John Campbell** on Blenheim, South Carolina: "The population's only eight. No...make that six. One guy died last week. And I'm outta town."

Chicago Cubs manager **Stan Hack** on Grand de Tour, Illinois: "It's so small we don't even have a town drunk. Everyone has to take his turn."

Detroit Lions coach **Monte Clark** on Kingsburg, California: "It's so small that the number one industry is taking bottles back to the store."

In 1958, a Senate Subcommittee under **Estes Kefauver** was seeking information on proposed legislation to exempt team sports from anti-trust laws. A lineup of baseball legends such as **Stan Musial** and **Ted Williams** were called to testify.

Yankee manager **Casey Stengel**, after 45 minutes of mind-numbing baffle-gab, left the subcommittee stunned. During one soaring solo of Stengelese, Kefauver finally interrupted: "Mr. Stengel, I'm not sure I made my question clear." To which Casey shot back: "Well that's all right. I'm not sure I am going to answer your question perfectly either." Which he didn't.

After his testimony, a **Sporting News** headline summed it up: **Casey Was Eloquent, But What Did He Say?** The senators didn't know either. Because, after 7,000 words of testimony, Stengel uttered not a *single* word about the proposed legislation.

But then, amazingly, **Mickey Mantle** — who testified next — upstaged him. In answer to Kefauver's first question, Mickey said, "Well sir, my views are about the same as Casey's."

While staying at the Antrim Lodge in the Catskills, fishing writer **Ed Zern** met a young chap who said he'd never caught a trout over 10 inches. So Zern took him out on the Beaverkill that afternoon, and the kid caught a fair-sized brown trout.

"That's a nice 15 or 16-inch fish," Zern beamed.

"Wow!" said the kid. "Sixteen inches."

"Maybe more," said Zern, to make him feel good.

Heading straight to the bar to celebrate, Zern told the other guests about the kid's catch. "How big was it?" the bartender asked.

"The kid said he hadn't measured it yet. But I'd say 16-17 inches."

"Hey," said a guy a few stools over, "I saw you catch it from the shore, and it looked even bigger than that."

"Well," grinned the kid, "could have *been*."

A few drinks later, Zern heard the kid describe his 18-inch trout. "Jeez," said another man, "I'd sure like to see it."

"Soon as I finish my drink," said the kid.

Zern sneaked off to the ice-locker, found the fish, and measured it. The trout was only 14 inches. Zern quickly stashed it with his own fish in the freezer. Just then, the others boiled in to view the famous trophy. "Gone," wailed the kid after a frantic search. "It's *gone*."

Then, turning to the crowd, he shrugged. "Well, if someone wants a 19-inch trout *that* bad, he's welcome to it."

After his reign as light heavyweight champ, **Archie Moore** kept making big bucks by public speaking. When an agent asked him which places he preferred to speak in, Archie said, "Prisons."

"Prisons," laughed the agent. "Why's that?"

"Because," said Archie, "*nobody* leaves before I'm finished."

Times sure have changed: When Brooklyn Dodgers' general manager **Branch Rickey** asked pitcher **Billy Loes** not to reveal the terms of the contract he'd just signed, Billy said, "Are you kidding? I'm just as ashamed of it as you are."

A golfer who was having a rotten day turned to his caddie and snarled, "You must be the world's worst caddie."

"I doubt it," shrugged the caddie. "That would be too much of a coincidence."

Besides being a pugilist, **Joe Louis** was also a philosopher. "Everybody wants to go to heaven," he observed, "but nobody wants to die to get there."

In **Bob Uecker's** very first game with the Braves in Milwaukee, he was walking to the batting cage when manager **Birdie Tebbetts** called him over. "Son," he said, "I know it's your hometown and all your relatives are here, but I don't wanna see ya so nervous."

Uecker insisted he was feeling just fine.

"Well in that case, kid, I should tell ya. Here in the big leagues, most of us wear our jockstraps *inside our uniforms.*"

Uecker, that irrepressible catcher in the wry, said baseball lore is filled with tearful tales of great players like Ruth and Mantle visiting hospitals, and then slugging homers for a sick little kid.

"I once made the same promise myself," Bob admitted. "Struck out three times, then discovered the kid was an out-patient."

The ballplayer-turned-broadcaster **Uecker** remembered when he signed with the Milwaukee Braves for $3,000. "It really bothered my dad at the time," he said, "since he'd never had that kind of dough. But eventually he scraped it up."

In his entire career, **Uecker** hit only 14 home runs. When he belted his first, he recalls, the fan in the stands who caught it threw it back.

A few seasons later, while playing the Giants, Uecker sent an entire stadium into shock by actually hitting a grand slam. When Giants manager **Herman Franks** stormed from the dugout to relieve pitcher **Ron Herbel,** he was carrying Herbel's suitcase.

But **Uecker** delivered his best line the day he got cut. "They broke it to me gently," he assured the press. "Before the game, the manager told me they didn't allow visitors in the clubhouse."

The guy's wife had been suspicious for weeks. But the night he rolled in at 2 a.m. and went straight to bed, she got mad. Pulling his little black book from his pocket, she flipped through it till she found a recent entry that read, "Maribelle Lee, 367-2521."

Shaking him awake, she jabbed the page and hollered, "Alright buster, who's this Maribelle Lee?"

The sly fox rubbed his eyes and moaned, "Not *who*, honey, *what*? Maribelle Lee was a long-shot filly at Aqueduct yesterday. Won by a nose in the sixth race."

"Yeah, *sure*!" she seethed. "So what's this 367...?"

"Hold it a second, hon," the rascal begged. "That's my bookie's address. He lives at 367 State street. I just wrote it down to remind me."

"Uh-huh," she snorted. "And the 2521?"

"Just read it slow, hon," he murmured. "25... 2... 1. It means twenty five to one. Maribelle Lee wasn't no sure thing, believe me. I'll tell ya the whole story in the morning." And seconds later he was snoring.

Completely confused, she climbed into bed and finally fell asleep. An hour later the phone rang.

She picked it up, listened with a look of stone cold fury, then whacked his head with the receiver.

"What is it now?" he wailed, whipping upright.

"It's for you," she hissed. "Your horse is on the phone."

Ranger goalie **Gump Worsley** and his coach **Phil Watson** formed a mutual animosity society. After one serious drubbing in Madison Square Garden, the irascible Watson blamed the team's loss on Worsley's drinking.

"How can we win, he bitched to the press, when our goalie has a beer belly?"

"It shows what a jerk we have for a coach," Gump scoffed. "I *just* drink Johnny Walker."

Wanting to contact Arizona State football star **Gary Bouck**, sportswriter **Jerry Guibor** called the team's equipment manager, **Chester Kropp**, and asked, "Do you happen to have Gary's number?"

"Jest hold on a minute," drawled the 73-year-old manager, setting down the phone. Guibor almost dozed off before Kropp shuffled back and said he had it.

"Great," sighed Guibor, "what's his number?"

"Sixty-five," said Kropp.

After retiring from baseball, Hall of Fame pitcher **Lefty Gomez** had a heart bypass operation. When a few old teammates visited him in the hospital, Lefty said, "Hell, if I'd known it was going to be *that* easy, I'd have had it when I was five."

In a bar one night, a writer asked major league pitcher **Tug McGraw** whether he preferred grass or AstroTurf.

"How should *I* know?" glowered Tug. "I never in my life smoked AstroTurf."

Standing in the divorce court, the outraged wife wailed, "From the day we got married, your honor, my husband hasn't cared about anything except playing the horses. He doesn't even remember our wedding anniversary."

"That's a lie," yelped her husband, jumping up. "I remember exactly when we got hitched. It was three days after Seattle Slew won the Preakness."

"Tell me honestly," a writer once asked **Gomez**, "did you ever throw a spitball?"

"Not intentionally," said Lefty. "But I *do* sweat easily."

It may not be golf's most hilarious line, but it's certainly one of the most astute. As pro golfer **Chi Chi Rodriguez** summed it up, "For most amateurs, the best wood in the bag is the pencil."

In no sport is cheating more common than with golfers. As the great **Arnie Palmer** said when asked if he had a tip to take strokes off anyone's game: "Sure I have a tip. It's called an eraser."

Perhaps the worst example of golfing skullduggery was observed by **Bob Bruce**. "A guy I played with cheated so badly that he once had a hole in one and wrote down zero on the scorecard."

Sportswriter **Jim Murray** tackled the same subject. "When finally," he wrote, "you get in the hole and start to mark your score, you say, 'I had a five there.' Then you look around, and if no one's looking back, you say, 'No, in fact, it was only a four.'

"In golf, this is known as improving your lie."

In 1983, when Soviet hockey star **Vladimir Krutov** was asked his impressions of **Wayne Gretzky**, he said Gretzky "isn't very fast" and that "his physique leaves much to be desired."

Krutov shoulda kept his yap shut. Six years later, when he moved to Vancouver to play with the Canucks, he was bloated.

Watching the tubby import grind up the ice, one of his teammates muttered, "Vlad can stickhandle past everything except a McDonald's."

Ted **Giannoulas** became famous with baseball fans as the guy inside the San Diego Chicken costume. A reporter once asked him if his mother didn't consider his job a bit foolish.

"Not at all," sniffed Ted. "She thinks I'm a doctor in Wisconsin."

During a night game in Boise, Idaho, **Rufus "Big Train" Johnson** was standing on first when a total power failure hit the park. Moments later, when the lights went back on, the Big Train was calmly standing on third.

Umpire **Marty Springstead's** initial major-league game haunted him for years. It was 1965 in Washington, when the Senators' strapping **Frank Howard** strode to the plate and got a knee-high pitch. "Strike!" shouted Springstead.

Howard instantly swiveled and fired a finger at the novice umpire's mask. "Listen buster," he snarled, "get something straight. I don't know where you came from, or what you're doing in the major leagues. But you don't call a strike on me with that pitch. *Understand*?"

Springstead meekly nodded.

When the second pitch whistled again past Howard's kneecap, the rattled ump shouted, "Two!"

Howard wheeled around. "Two *what?*" he shrieked.

"Too *low*, Frank," squeaked Springstead. "*Much* too low."

Howard, however, wasn't always so intimidating. Once, while playing with the Los Angeles Dodgers, the big outfielder reached first base on a walk.

Since the secret signal for the hit-and-run was to call out the baserunner's surname, the first-base coach **Pete Reiser** shouted, "Okay Howard, on your toes. Be ready for anything *Howard*."

Howard called time, and ambled over to Reiser. "Hey Pete," he said, "we're pals. Call me Frank."

After a week of hunting in Sudbury, Ontario, the three big bruisers drove back to Toronto and headed into a saloon. The rest of the night, they sat at the bar and raved about the wonders of the northern town.

Finally, the barman had endured enough. "Jeez, knock it off," he snarled. "Only two things ever came outta Sudbury – hookers and hockey players."

There was total silence until one man stood slowly and jutted his chin across the bar. "Oh yeah?" he growled. "My sister comes from Sudbury."

The barman paused only a second. "No kidding?" he chirped. "What position does she play?"

Making no bones about his delinquent youth, Middleweight champ **Rocky Graziano** frankly admitted, "We stole anything that began with *a* – *a* banana, *a* bicycle, *a* watch..."

As for school, "I quit in the sixth grade because of pneumonia. Not because I had it, but because I couldn't spell it."

When it came to childhood poverty, golfer **Lee Trevino** could out-boast the best of them. "My family was so poor," he said, "they couldn't afford any kids. The lady next door had me."

Jake LaMotta was another Middleweight champ whose boyhood was less than beatific. "We were so poor," he said, "my old man would go out every Christmas Eve and shoot his gun, then come in and tell us Santa had committed suicide."

When a rookie ballplayer showed up late on his first day of practice, his coach stormed over and shouted in his face, "You shoulda been here at nine o'clock!"

"*Really?*" chirped the rookie. "Why, what happened?"

One wickedly cold night, two besotted buddies decided to go fishing. After chopping holes in the ice, they dropped their lines and waited. Ten minutes later, a voice boomed down from above, "There are no fish in there."

The startled men stared wildly around, but when they saw no one they carried on. Five minutes later, the voice boomed down again: "I told you, there are no fish in there."

Terrified, one of the men looked up and squeaked, "Are you God?"

"No," growled the voice. "I'm the rink superintendent."

During World War II, when hockey stars were at a premium, **Thomas "Windy" O'Neill** played for the Toronto Maple Leafs. Some considered him more adept at playing the piano. But besides his skills on the ice and keyboard, Windy was also a lawyer who was running for the Ontario Legislature.

One evening, Windy rushed into a campaign meeting and tossed off his coat. Then, after making an impassioned speech, he discovered his coat had been stolen. But what bothered him most was the pair of hockey tickets he'd put in a pocket.

The police had no clue who'd taken the coat — until one cop joked, "Maybe the thief's just dumb enough to use the tickets." They laughed, until a Sergeant said, "Well, it's worth checking out." Sure enough, they arrested the guy in Windy's seat at the game that night — an unemployed Black man who lived in the riding Windy was running for.

When the story hit the papers, Windy soon was deluged with irate calls from other Black constituents. The man was poor, they said, and had no previous record. If Windy persisted in prosecuting, he wouldn't get their votes.

So Windy asked the cops to drop the charge. "No way," they said. "*You* laid the charge. And we nailed him."

Windy was distraught. When the case came up, he was in the courtroom when the charge was read. The judge looked down and said, "Mr. O'Neill, I understand you're the complainant in this case."

Windy jumped to his feet and thundered, "No, Your Honor. Absolutely *not*! I happen to represent the accused."

Umpire **Tom Gorman** once explained that if a team in a dugout riled him so much that he had to storm over to the bench, he *had* to toss some player out to save face. But, he added, in order not to hurt the team, he usually picked a guy who'd pitched the day before and wouldn't be called that day.

One afternoon in Ebbets Field, the Dodgers' bench kept razzing Gorman incessantly. So, while chugging toward the dugout, he remembered **John Van Cuyk** had pitched the day before. Pointing at the team in general, he snorted, "You're outta here, Van Cuyk."

Brooklyn manager **Chuck Dressen** shouted back, "*Who* ya want out?"

"Van *Cuyk*," Gorman hollered.

"That's great," Chuck smiled, "but you'll have to yell a little louder."

"What the hell for?" raged Gorman.

"Cause I sent him back to the Texas League last night."

Jockey **Mary Bacon** never forgot the race she rode on a mare in foal — six days before giving birth herself. "I'll always feel sorry for those fans who bet on a pregnant horse ridden by a pregnant jockey," she recalled.

"The four of us finished last."

When **Bill Veeck** owned the St. Louis Browns, he had a terrible time attracting crowds to the ballpark. Once, after inviting someone to a game, the guy asked, "What time does it start?"

"Hey," shrugged Veeck, "what time's *convenient?*"

Before Northern Dancer was retired from the track, he'd won more money than any horse on earth. Yet only two years before his peak racing season, Dancer's owner, **Edward Plunkett Taylor**, had offered to sell him for $25,000.

Horse owner **Larkin Maloney** and his trainer, **Carl Chapman**, considered purchasing the colt, but decided to sink their money into another, subsequently mediocre, nag instead. Thus, Taylor kept Northern Dancer.

And for years, Chapman was derided for missing out on the galloping goldmine. Yet during his dotage, when the subject was raised, Chapman finally snorted, "Why the hell ya knocking *me*? Did ya ever ask why E.P. Taylor tried to sell that horse for a measly twenty-five grand?"

Actor **John Wayne** said he gave up bowling because, "very few alleys let me come back.... I had an overhand delivery."

Following a news report that he'd died, featherweight boxing champ **Willie Pep** told the press, "Nah, I didn't die last night. In fact, I didn't even leave the house."

After his California Angels lost a game, owner **Gene Autry** told a reporter, "You know that Grantland Rice once said, 'It's not whether you win or lose, but how you play the game?'"

"Yeah," said the scribe, "I *knew* that."

"Well," growled Autry, "as far as I'm concerned, Grantland Rice can go to hell."

During an exhibition game with the Sabres, Toronto Maple Leaf forward **John Kordic** was pointed to the penalty box. While sitting there steaming, he saw Buffalo coach **Rick Dudley** – proudly sporting his ill-disguised toupée – smirking at him. That did it.

"Hey, Dudley!" Kordic screamed, "the next time your cat dies, *bury* it – don't *wear* it."

Not all great athletes are egocentrics. As Detroit Lions' defensive tackle **Alex Karras** gleefully admitted, "I never graduated from Iowa. I was only there for two terms – Truman's and Eisenhower's.

When **Rickey Henderson** threatened to write a tell-all book about the New York Yankees, **Dallas Green** snorted, "Before he writes a book, he should read one."

Even after her divorce from **Pete Rose**, ex-wife **Karolyn** still harbored certain sympathy. "You've got to give him *some* credit for what he's accomplished," she insisted. "He never went to college, and the only book he ever read was **The Pete Rose Story**."

Florida football coach **Steve Spurrier** sadly announced that a fire at Auburn's football dorm had destroyed 20 books.

"But the real tragedy," he added, "is that 15 hadn't been colored yet."

In both the brawn and brains departments, Florida state football coach **Bobby Bowden** had his linebacker, **Reggie Herring,** pretty well summed up. "Reggie doesn't know the meaning of the word fear," Bowden said. "In fact, I just looked at his grades — and he doesn't know the meaning of most words."

At the winter Olympics in Lake Placid, famed Canadian skier **Ken Read** was the leading contender for a downhill gold medal. With one successful run, it was his.

At the starting signal, he blasted from the gate to a massive cheer — and within one second, was struck with horror. That's how long it took him to realize he'd only snapped one ski on.

On his very first hole, golfer **Ron Clare** sliced his ball into the woods, then shanked one across the roadway, blasted into a sandtrap, and then landed back in the woods. After half an hour, his frustrated partner snorted, "Hey, why doncha just forget it and drop another one?"

"You *kidding*?" Clare growled. "It's my lucky ball."

Upon taking over the newly franchised New York Mets in 1962, manager **Casey Stengel** growled at his pack of rookies, "Awright, line up alphabetically by height."

Before rookie **Cecil Dillon** signed his contract with the New York Rangers, veteran players told him it would be wise to tell manager **Lester Patrick** he was actually a year younger in order to stay longer in the league.

Dillon gratefully agreed.

After the negotiations, a player asked, "So Dill, did you remember to deduct a year?"

"Sure did," he beamed. "Told him I was born in 1907 instead of 1908."

A fanatic golfer was putting on a green, surrounded by six bored caddies. Since the golf-nut always played alone, a friend who saw him was puzzled. Sauntering over, he asked, "Hey Phil, what's going on?"

"Blame the wife," scowled Phil, tapping his putt. "She insisted I spend more time with the kids."

After his divorce, hockey great **Bobby Hull** conceded, "My wife made me a millionaire. I *used* to have three million."

The ballplayer asked the owner to give him a big raise.

"Why?" asked the owner.

"So I can go," the player said, "somewhere I've never been."

"Ahhh," said the owner. "You mean third base."

When country singer **Willie Nelson** purchased a golf course near Austin, Texas, a reporter asked what the total par was.

"Any dang thing I want it to be," Willie drawled. "For instance, this hole right here's a par 47 — and yesterday I birdied the sucker."

Unlike Europe, where nations nearly go to war during soccer playoffs, the sport in North America hasn't exactly spurred cataclysmic events. But Washington Diplomats player **Paul Cannell** tried. During one game, he shocked the stands by stripping off his shorts – then afterwards explained to police, "Hey, I was just trying to give the sport a little more exposure."

As a hockey star, **Eddie Shore** was brilliant, but as owner of the Springfield club, he was bizarre. He tied a player's legs together because he said they were too far apart. He tied a goalie to the crossbar to teach him to stand up straight. After a losing game, he locked the ref in the dressing room. And one day, he invited the players' wives to the arena. When they all flocked in expecting a surprise party, he sat them down and ordered them to "be celibate — at least till the playoffs are over."

Then there was the time he traded for a player named Smith. When the guy arrived in the dressing room, Shore snarled, "Where the hell are your goal pads?"

"Goal pads?" frowned Smith.

"Yah, *goal* pads," barked Shore. "*Every* goalie has goal pads, dammit."

"But," said Smith, "I'm a forward."

A Missouri newspaper editor was furious at local sports publicist **Bill Callahan** for always getting names wrong.

"You're right," agreed Bill. "I *used* to have a terrible time remembering names — but I'm okay now."

"Yeah?" scoffed the newsman. "Since *when*?"

"Well," beamed Bill, "ever since I took that Dan Carnegie course."

When Houston Astro executive **Don Davidson** was asked about hyperactive pitcher Joe Niekro's inability to relax, Davidson said, "Well, let's put it this way. It takes Joe two hours to watch '60 Minutes.'"

Every Canadian sports nut remembers **Paul Henderson** scoring the final goal in the famous Team Canada match against Russia. But how many recall **Phil Esposito's** magic moment in the Forum?

It was the night the series began. The announcer was introducing the Canadian players. As their names were called, they shot onto the ice individually to take the applause of the crowd.

Then, as the speakers boomed, "And *now*, one of the greatest hockey stars in history, Philll Esposiiiiito!" the cheers were deafening. Phil jumped from the bench and shot out of the gate — then did a complete cartwheel, landing smack on his back.

For the only time in his entire career, he sheepishly told the press, he'd forgotten to take off his skate guards.

When Los Angeles Angels' owner **Gene Autry** was asked about his Brooklyn Dodgers' counterpart **Walter O'Malley**, the old celluloid cowboy said, "There's nothin' in the world I wouldn't do for Walter, and there's nothin' he wouldn't do for me. We go through life doing nothin' for each other."

After his 916th game as the Alabama basketball coach, **Wimp Sanderson** was asked by a rookie reporter how many years he'd been there. "Well," said Wimp, "I'll tell ya son, when I got here the Dead Sea wasn't even sick."

Because Boston Bruin forward **Terry O'Reilly** played golf every Sunday, his wife was concerned for his soul. So going to her parish priest, she asked, "Father, is it a sin for Terry to play on the Sabbath?"

"Ahh, Mrs. O'Reilly," said the priest, "the way Terry golfs, it's a sin for him to play *any* day of the week."

When **Lake Kelly** was the Oral Roberts' basketball coach, he admitted to facing certain problems at the deeply fundamentalist college. "If you're going to the Final Four," he groaned, "yuh gotta recruit athletes, *not* Christians."

The Milwaukee Brewers had a long tradition of celebrating team birthdays with lavish fetes before a game. So just before manager **"Jolly" Charlie Grimm's** big day came due, his boss, **Bill Veeck**, asked what he'd like as a present.

"A good left-handed pitcher," grumped Grimm. Veeck howled.

On the day of his birthday, a giant cake was toted to the pitcher's mound where Grimm was given a $1,000 savings bond. But when Charlie started sawing the cake with a sword, Veeck suddenly grabbed his arm. And just then a guy jumped out of the cake.

"Who the hell's *this*?" yelped the startled Grimm.

"Julie Acosta," grinned Veeck. "I just bought him from Norfolk for $7,500. He's a left-handed pitcher."

During World War II, the New York Rangers' **Steve Buzinski** was tending goal in Maple Leaf Gardens when, during a flurry around the net, Toronto's **Bob Davidson** glanced a puck off his forehead. Though the wound was minor, Buzinski, seemingly unconscious, slumped to the ice.

His teammates were irate. "Hey, didja *see* that?" Ranger **Ott Heller** roared at the ref. "Davidson was high-sticking."

"That's crap," snorted Bob. "He got hit by the *puck*."

"The *stick*!" screamed Heller.

"The *puck*!" bellowed Bob.

At that point, Buzinski elbowed up and shouted, "He hit me with the *stick*." Then, instantly, he returned to his coma.

President **Calvin Coolidge** was blamed for many things. But no one ever accused him of being a football fan. Once at a White House reception, Senator McKinley of Illinois ushered a gridiron great over to Coolidge. "Mr. President," the senator said, "I'd like you to meet Red Grange who plays with the Bears."

Coolidge shook Red's hand and said, "Nice to meet you, young man. I've always liked animal acts."

After baseball commissioner **Bowie Kuhn** gave the 52 released Iranian hostages lifetime passes to major league baseball games, CBS Sports publicist **Beano Cook** muttered, "Good Lord. Haven't they suffered enough?"

The two bitter rivals at Pennsylvania's Lehigh Country Club argued so consistently that they finally agreed not to speak at all when playing. As months went by, the silence was serene.

But then one day on the sixteenth hole, Sam found himself in a sandtrap.

Doc waited patiently as Sam took a chop with his nine iron. Then another. Then another. Until, finally, he topped a shot clear across the green — which landed in a trap on the other side.

After four more furious swings, he lobbed the ball across the green into trap number one again.

As Sam stomped back across the grass, Doc finally muttered, "May I say one thing?"

"What the hell is it?" snarled Sam.

"Well," said Doc, "you're playing with my ball."

On the day of **Howard Cosell's** loquacious debut as an ABC sports commentator, network president **Roone Arledge** called him after the broadcast. "Cosell," he barked, "get one thing straight. We're not paying you by the syllable."

When asked why he was named football coach at California despite having no experience, former NFL quarterback **Joe Kapp** fired back: "Well, if Howard Cosell can coach 28 NFL teams each week, I figure I can coach one college team."

Indeed, few athletes were enamored with **Cosell.**

Racer **Jackie Stewart** said, "In one year, I travelled 450,000 miles by air. That's 18 times around the world, or once around Howard's head."

Once, when the infamous motormouth admitted that he was his own worst enemy, **Irving Rudd** said, "Not while *I'm* alive."

And in one of his few more logical moments, **Muhummad Ali** said, "I often wish that I was a dog and Cosell was a fire hydrant."

Bob and **Barclay Plager**, the St. Louis Blues' battling brothers, could handle their dukes as dexterously as their sticks. And mostly, they slugged each other. The sibling rivalry started when they were kids in Kirkland Lake, Ontario, and lasted into junior hockey.

One night in Guelph, Ontario, Barclay stuck his stick between Bob's teeth. Bob hauled off and whacked him on the skull. In the penalty box, the punch-up continued. Tossed out of the game, they battled all the way to the dressing rooms. When the match finally ended, they were still going at it.

After their teammates finally pried them apart, Bob stormed off to a diner near the rink. Ten minutes later, Barclay strode in — trailed by the entire Guelph team. Bob stood up, fists clenched, as his sibling approached. Then the entire room hushed in horrified expectation as Barclay grabbed his brother by the shoulder.

"Hey Bob," he mumbled, "could ya lend me five bucks?"

Aside from fighting, defenceman **Bob Plager** adored practical jokes. On one team flight he snipped off the tie of the snoozing **Sid Salomon III** – the St. Louis Blue's president. So, during practice the next day, Sid III cut off the legs of Bob's new slacks.

But after Plager refused payment for the pants, Sid III invited him to a formal soiree he was hosting.

Plager promised he'd show up – and *did,* wearing the same pair of scissored slacks.

As the tuxedoed guests gasped, Plager held out his hand. "Okay Sid," he said, "*now* I'll take your check."

Salomon shoulda done his homework. **Bob Plager** was nuts.

Before signing with the Blues, he'd played with the New York Rangers. One day, he sauntered into the office of the Rangers' publicist, **John Halligan**, and calmly lifted a portable radio off his desk.

"I thought he only wanted it for a few days in his hotel," Halligan later confessed. "But when I asked him a week later where it was, he said, "Oh, *that!* I just mailed it home to my mother."

After straying from their buddy in the woods, two hunters realized they were hopelessly lost. Then Zeke had a sudden brainwave. "Hey, Fred," he said, "why don't ya fire a shot in the air?"

"Jeez," said Fred. "I shoulda thought a that myself." So he aimed a shot straight up.

By sunset, when nothing happened, Zeke said, "Well Fred, seems they didn't hear us. You better fire off another." So Fred did. And once again, nothing.

When the moon began rising, Zeke started to panic. "Dang it, Fred," he growled, "shoot off one more."

Fred shook his head. "Can't," he said, "I'm out of arrows."

At the sound of the eight bell, the boxer wobbled back to his corner and sagged into his manager's arms.

Lowering him gently onto the stool, the manager pleaded, "Just try to hang on for another round, Slugger. I think what he's doing to you is beginning to sicken him."

At the end of the sixth round, a bruised and bloody boxer staggered to his corner and collapsed on the stool.

While daubing his cuts with a septic stick, his manager kept shouting in his ear, "He's not hurting you! He's not hurting you!"

The boxer groaned. "Then keep your eye on the referee. **Somebody's** beating the crap outta me."

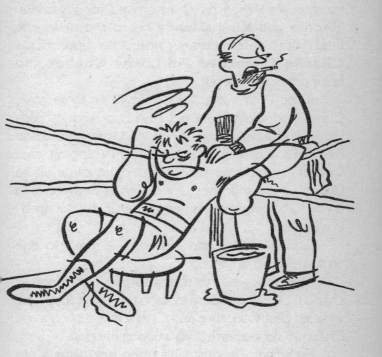

New York Americans' winger **Eddy Convey** was warned he'd be sent to the minors if he didn't score more goals. When his team arrived for a game in Toronto and **King Clancy** heard the news, the Leafs' star defenceman cajoled his teammates **Charlie Conacher** and **Lorne Chabot** into helping their buddy out.

If the Leafs were ahead by two or three goals, Clancy said, the trio should ease back and let Eddy score. And sure enough, when the Leafs were ahead by three, Convey got the puck. Whipping past Conacher, who seemed distracted, he came up to Clancy, who suddenly stumbled. Then Eddy bore in on the Leaf net, where goalie Lorne Chabot lounged in a corner.

Convey shot – and missed by a mile. No one could believe it.

Clancy begged his mates to give Eddy another chance. So when Convey got the puck again, he whizzed past Conacher and Clancy and zeroed in on Chabot, who was practically hugging the post.

Eddy shot – and hit Chabot on his Adam's apple.

The goalie slumped gasping to the ice. "That's *it,*" he croaked when King and Charlie skated up. "Screw charity! That moron don't deserve to score."

Because of a top scorer named **Dick Roberge**, the Johnstown Jets were the hottest team in the Eastern League. In a game against New Haven, the Jets were leading 8-0 when Roberge blasted through the Blade defense to score his fifth goal.

As the local fans went berserk with rage, the New Haven coach started gasping. This wasn't murder — it was massacre. So the next time he saw Roberge wind up from his own net and start sizzling down the ice, the coach stood and screamed, "Awright, *EVERY-BODY* out!"

And he *meant* it. Emptied his bench. Sent all 14 players into the game.

When the ref shrilled his whistle and demanded an explanation, the coach simply shrugged. "I just wanted to see if the sumbitch could skate through my *entire* team and score."

A keen young golfer was waiting at a tee as an old duffer in front of him lined up his shot. Suddenly the young man noticed that the old guy's ball was sitting a foot in front of the tee-off blocks. "Excuse me for interrupting sir," he said, "but your ball's supposed to be in line with the markers – or behind them."

The old geezer turned and glowered. "Thanks very much for the information, son. Now, do you mind shutting up while I take my second shot?"

When **Bob "Hound" Kelly** played for the Philadelphia Flyers, his roommate **Wayne Hillman** constantly belittled Hound's I.Q. One sopping Sunday morning after church, Hound stomped into their apartment and smirked at Hillman. "Hey wise guy, you always call me dumb. But it's pouring rain, and your car's outside with the windows open."

"So, dammit," Hillman growled, "why didn't you close them?"

"I *couldn't,*" frowned Hound. "The doors were locked."

Sportswriter **Emmett Watson** once wrote a column warning parents:

"Never raise your son to be a football coach. In fact, if he ever expresses the desire to be one, stop raising him."

New York third baseman **Graig Nettles** once told a writer, "As a kid I wanted either to be a baseball player or join the circus. When I signed with the Yankees I finally did both."

Philbert loved playing the ponies, but hardly ever won. One day he went to the bookie with his last two dollars and said, "Put it on Bayside on the fifth."

"Hey Philbert," begged the bookie, "stop wasting your money. The odds on the nag are 150 to 1. It ain't got a chance."

But Philbert persisted.

"Look," said the bookie, "the horse simply *cannot* win. I'll personally give you a million-to-one odds on him. Whaddaya say about that?"

"I'll take it," said Philbert. And, of course, Bayside won.

Philbert returned to his bookie's with a suitcase. But even as he stuffed it with bills, he still looked sad.

"I don't get it," said the bookie. "You've just won a fortune, and don't even seem pleased."

"Why *should* I be?" Philbert grumbled. "I've been betting all my life and hardly won a cent. So finally I hit on a million-to-one shot. And what have I got on it? A stinking two bucks."

Maple Leafs boss **Conn Smythe** knew his arch rival, **Art Ross**, the Bruins owner, had just undergone a hemorrhoid operation. So one night on his way to the Boston Stadium, Smythe bought a dozen roses from a vendor. Just prior to the game, Smythe asked his defenceman, King Clancy, to deliver the roses to Ross.

Clancy skated over to where Ross was sitting with a group of Brahmnin Bostonians and handed him the bouquet – along with an accompanying card inscribed in Latin. Ross was deeply touched by Smythe's thorny present, and especially the note which he couldn't read.

Thanking Clancy, he then handed the roses to the blue-blooded lady beside him. The lady, who *could* read Latin, beamed with pleasure, read the note, then gasped in horror.

The message read: "YOU KNOW WHERE TO SHOVE THESE."

A husband left home at every opportunity, claiming he was going golfing. One afternoon while he was away, his wife was horrified to discover a box of miniskirts, blouses, and pantyhose hidden in his closet.

Rushing next door she blurted out the story to her neighbor, sobbing, "I just don't know where I went wrong."

"Hey," said her friend, "it's nothing to get upset about. Everyone knows Jack will do anything to hit from the ladies' tee."

When the New York Yankees visited Puerto Rico on a promotional tour, the Don Q Rum company hosted a banquet for the players. Because the party was being broadcast, the team asked sports reporter **Red Smith** to reply to the constant toasts. Red managed magnificently, but kept referring to his hosts as "the makers of that wonderful Bacardi rum."

Finally, an irate Don Q official jumped up and shouted, "Don Q, Senor. *Don Q.*"

"You're welcome," beamed Red. "You're *welcome!*"

Pro golfer-turned-bowler **Don Carter** once explained why he'd decided to switch games. "One of the advantages," he said, "is that you rarely lose a bowling ball."

You think current hockey is violent?

Let's zap back to January 14, 1911 in Northern Ontario. Cobalt's star center, **Harry Smith**, was facing the Haileybury team. In the first ten minutes of the game, Smith smashed the nose of a guy named Johnston, and spent five minutes on the bench.

Back on the ice, he loosened two teeth of a guy named Morrison, and got five minutes more.

Back on the ice, he brained a guy named Corbeau. But when referee **George Gwynne** aimed him again at the penalty box, Smith axed Gwynne with his stick on the mouth, snapping two teeth. That's when, by crowd demand, Smith was finally arrested.

At his trial, he was fined $25 and costs. The magistrate said that if referee Gwynne was there to lay charges, Smith would have rotted in jail. Smith paid up and shot out the door — seconds before Gwynne bolted in from the dentist's.

The judge gave Gwynne sheer hell for being late. "Dammit," he stormed, "who cares about your teeth? *I* could have chewed him alive if you'd been here."

Riding the rails with the Cardinals, sportswriter **Grantland Rice** was interviewing **Dizzy Dean** and his brother Daffy – who was swigging a soda. When the train shot into a tunnel, Rice swore he heard Daffy hiss in the darkness, "Hey, Diz, did ya drunk any of this stuff yet?"

"Nope," drawled the dizzy one.

"Then *don't!*" muttered Daffy. "*I* just did. And I've gone plumb blind."

Bonked on the skull by a blistering fastball in the 1934 World Series, St. Louis Cardinals pitcher **Dizzy Dean** proudly informed sportswriters: "The doctors X-rayed my head, and found absolutely nothing."

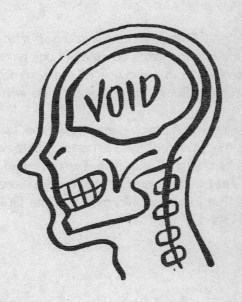

After retiring, **Dean** became a radio sportscaster. Noticing a fracas in the stands during a St. Louis game, Diz told his listeners: "I don't know what the commotion's about down there. But it's got somethin' to do with a fat lady."

When a horrified station executive said the "fat lady" was, in fact, the Queen of the Netherlands, Dizzy asked where the Netherlands was. The executive told him.

"Oh," said Diz, and went back to his mike. "Sorry," he apologized. "I've just been informed that the fat lady's Queen of Holland."

Notre Dame coach **Frank Leahy** harbored serious homicidal impulses when he grabbed his quarterback, **Johnny Lujack**, and asked him why the hell he'd thrown three interceptions to Army's **Arnold Tucker**.

Leahy had to be physically restrained when Lujack shrugged: "Hey coach, he was the *only* man open."

Oakland Raiders' guard **Don Manoukian** liked his steaks extremely rare. So rare, in fact, that when a waiter asked him how he'd like it, he said, "Hell, just knock the breath out of it."

Pro golfer **Tom Bolt** got his nickname "Terrible Tommy" because of his fierce temper on the fairways – where he frequently re-shaped his clubs into pretzels around trees. Once, approaching a green from 125 yards, his caddie suggested a two-iron.

"A **two**-iron?" Bolt exploded. "Why?"

"Well, sir," said the caddie, "it's the only one still in your bag."

Even sanguine golfer **Sam Snead** nearly encircled his caddie in an iron once. Approaching the 16th hole at Firestone, with a pond in front of the green, Snead asked his caddie which club he'd suggest. "Well," said the guy, "yesterday I caddied for Jay Herbert, and he used an 8-iron."

So Sam grabbed his 8-iron — and promptly lofted the ball smack into the pond. Wheeling on the caddie, he hissed, "Are you *sure* Herbert hit an 8 here?"

"Yes sir, he did," the caddie swore.

"And *where*," asked Snead, "did it land?"

"Same place," piped the caddie. "In the pond."

Asked about his golf game, comedian **Joe E. Lewis** rasped, "I *always* play in the low 80s." Then, after pausing, he said, "If it gets any hotter, I won't play."

Writer **Bernard Darwin**:

"Golf is not a funeral – though both can be very sad affairs."

Snead has had other moments of frustration. He was golfing with a pal named Nixon at West Virginia's Greenbrier when his buddy landed in a thicket. "No one," Sam said, "could shoot out of it without a bazooka. I figured he was going to drop another ball, take his loss like anyone else, and play on. But hell no. He disappears in there, and seconds later his ball flies onto the fairway. Nixon comes out looking real pleased as punch.

"I knew he threw it," Snead continued, "but what could I say? After all, he *was* the President."

After a game with the Senators in Ottawa, the New York Rangers decided to celebrate their victory in nearby Hull. But before they headed off, en masse, across the Quebec border, their militant manager **Lester Patrick** aimed a finger. "Just remember the one o'clock curfew," he barked. "Be back on the pullman not a second later."

Sometime before sunrise, the players staggered back. But before climbing aboard, **Leo Bourgeault** turned to **Butch Keeling** and murmured, "For godsakes, be quiet. *Don't* wake Lester."

"Yah," nodded Keeling, and turning to the guy behind him hissed, "Don't wake Lester." The warning was mumbled down the line.

Late the following morning, Leo groped his way to the diner to see Lester finishing breakfast. "Good morning, Mr. Bourgeault," Lester said icily. Leo sheepishly nodded back.

"By the way," the manager added, "did you know your friend Mr. Keeling walks in his sleep?"

Leo shook his throbbing head, and muttered, "No sir."

"Well he *does!*" seethed Lester. "Just before dawn, Mr. Keeling crept into my compartment and started urinating on the floor. Then, when I shouted, 'What the hell are you doing?' the moron put his fingers to his lips, and whispered, 'Shhhhh. Don't wake Lester.'"

In the depths of the Depression, **Babe Ruth** was asked to take the first salary cut of his career. Babe flatly refused, insisting on his usual $80,000 contract.

"But Babe," a Yankee official protested, "times are tough. That's more dough than Hoover made last year as President."

"Yah, I know," snapped Ruth. "But I had a better year than Hoover."

Even more than smacking homers, **Ruth** loved to cavort all night — which drove **Miller Huggins**, his manager, mad. But even though he could berate ordinary players for staying out late, Miller found it hard to chastise baseball's greatest superstar.

One night, when Babe was still A.W.O.L. from his hotel at 3 a.m., Huggins told a reporter, "I swear, I'm gonna settle this once and for all. Just watch!"

At that exact second, Ruth swaggered into the lobby.

"There he is," nudged the reporter. "Ya gonna have words with him?"

"You're damn right." said Huggins. "Well, hi ya, Babe."

In a game against Philadelphia, Montreal Expos' manager **Dick Williams** ordered an intentional walk to **Bake McBride** with runners on second and third.

Then the Phillies' **Mike Schmidt** promptly hit a single to win the game.

Minutes later, in the locker room, the red-faced Williams defended his strategy. "I don't care if Jesus Christ was coming up," he grumped. "I was going to walk McBride."

"Oh yeah," asked a reporter, "what if Babe Ruth was coming up?"

Williams shuffled his feet a moment, then murmured, "Well...I'm not so sure about Babe."

On the Echo Lake golf course, novelist **Bud Kelland** had a near-perfect drive — till his ball plunked into a trap two feet from the green. His three companions, out of sight, heard him whacking away for two minutes.

When his ball finally popped onto the green, one of his pals asked, "How many shots did you have in there, Bud?"

"Four," Bud grumped.

"That's strange," grinned his buddy, "the rest of us heard eight."

"Well, dammit," snorted Bud, "remember where ya *are*! Four of them were echoes."

Red Sox pitcher **Bill Lee** was never a player to suffer sportswriters gladly. In the first game of the 1975 World Series, the Sox beat Cincinnati 6-0. After the second game, which the Reds won 3 to 2, a writer asked Lee to sum up the series so far.

Lee stared back for a solid 30 seconds before he said, "It's tied."

An editor of the **Dallas News** once banned the use of all nicknames such as 'Bobby,' 'Charlie,' and 'Tommy.' And so, the following day, a football writer dutifully reported: "Doak Walker has been sidelined by a Charles horse."

Two golf-mad oldsters were playing together in Palm Springs when a funeral cortege rolled past. One of them saw the line of cars and instantly dropped his club. Then, whipping off his cap, he stood erect until the procession passed.

"Jeez, Sam," said his friend, "I've never seen you interrupt a game for *anything* before."

"Well," shrugged Sam, "it's the least I could do. After all, I was married to her for thirty years."

Ballplayer **George Pipgras** never forgot the first time he batted against **Walter Johnson.** After two strikes, Pipgras stepped off the plate and said to catcher **Muddy Ruel**, "I never even *saw* those pitches."

"Don't let it worry you," Muddy soothed. "He's thrown some Ty Cobb's still looking for."

Lefty Gomez was also a pitcher whose fastball terrified most batters – except for **Jimmie Foxx.** Even Lefty admitted he had trouble with the legendary power hitter.

Once, with Foxx at bat, catcher **Bill Dickey** gave Gomez signal after signal – but Lefty kept shaking each one off. Finally, in exasperation, Dickey jogged to the mound and demanded, "Well, what exactly *do* you wanna throw him?"

"I don't wanta throw him *nothin'*," muttered Gomez. "Maybe he'll just get tired of waitin' and leave."

Ohio State football coach **Woody Hayes** said he once recruited a Czech kicker who was asked during an eye examination if he could read the bottom line.

"Read it!" the Czech yelped. "I *know* him!"

As a novice basketball coach with LaSalle, **Speedy Morris** recalls his elation when his wife said **Sports Illustrated** was calling. "So I cut myself shaving and tumble down the stairs in my rush to the phone. And the voice on the other end said, "For just 75 cents an issue..."

After being hit by lightning at the 1975 Western Open, **Lee Trevino** gasped, "My whole life flashed before me – and I couldn't believe how bad it was."

Still, Trevino swore he'd never be bolted by lightning again. "I'll just walk to the clubhouse holding a one-iron over my head. Even God can't hit a one-iron."

Hockey star **Ron Ellis** recalls this story. In the heyday of the Philly-Boston feud, the Bruins right-winger **Wayne Cashman** and his teammates emerged victorious from a particularly vicious feud and flocked to a tavern to celebrate.

But one drink led to 10, and a bar-room brawl broke out. The cops were called, and the bellicose Bruins were arrested.

In the hoosegow, Cashman hollered, "I demand my rights."

"And just *what* rights," asked the jailer, "do you *want?*"

"Is it true," asked Wayne, "I can make one phone call?"

When the guard said yes, Cashman nodded. "Okay, I wanna make one."

"Fine," said the guard, and led him to a pay phone. After fumbling through the directory for ten minutes, Cashman beamed, "Hey, I think I found a guy."

"Terrific," smiled the guard, a Bruins fan. "I hope he's good cause this is your only call."

"No sweat," winked Wayne, and dialed.

When the phone was answered, Cashman burbled, "Hey great, you're still open. I wanna order eight pizzas to go."

Dallas Cowboys', quarterback **Don Meredith** once complained about his coach **Tom Landry:** "He's such a *perfectionist.* If he married Raquel Welch, he'd expect her to cook."

When asked if his coach, **Tom Landry**, ever smiled, former Dallas fullback **Walt Garrison** said, "I don't know. I only played there nine years."

Major league outfielder **Pat Kelly** was a born-again Christian. Talking one day to his manager, Earl Weaver, Kelly asked, "Aren't you glad I walk with the Lord, Earl?"

Answered Weaver, "I'd rather you walked with the bases loaded."

Before **John Garrett** became a hockey broadcaster, he tended goal for the Hartford Whalers. One night, in Washington, a Capital player slashed such a dazzling shot past his pads that Garrett couldn't believe it.

So, to check out the replay, he stood gaping at the huge scoreboard screen dangling above center ice. But during his perusal, play was resumed – and the Caps' **Mike Gartner** took a pass and smacked a slapshot.

Garrett's eyes were still glued to the screen when he heard his teammates screaming. Glancing down, he saw the puck whizzing past him into the macrame.

Two goals in ten seconds were enough for coach **Don Blackburn**. Waving Garrett over, he jabbed a finger at the bench. "Okay, that's *it*!" he snarled. "You can watch the next replay from here."

Of the gaggle of "pro" wrestlers who toured Ontario weekly in the 1970s, one of the biggest draws was a mysterious hulk billed as "The Masked Marvel." When fans began demanding to know his identity, the promoters dreamed up a new hype. "On the first night he loses," they promised, "the Masked Marvel will be instantly unmasked."

Yet weeks went by as the masked one continued to win. And then, one exceedingly dull Monday in the city of North Bay, the Marvel — incognito in civvies — hit a downtown tavern with his opponent of that evening, **Al "Bunny" Dunlop**. After spending the entire afternoon in the bar, the Marvel, unlike Bunny, got royally soused.

That night at the fight, the hooded hero, horrendously hungover, barely staggered to the ring — where, for the first three minutes, Bunny struggled valiantly just to hold him up. But when the Marvel finally slipped from his grasp and crashed to the mat, Bunny swiftly straddled his opponent's back. Then, to his horror, he heard the Marvel snore.

"Hell," Bunny thought, "if the idiot doesn't get up, I'll win. And they'll have to unmask him."

Which, as Bunny later stated, was unthinkable — since the planned scenario called for the Marvel to be unmasked the following *Thursday* in Toronto's Maple Leaf Gardens. *(cont'd next page)*

Bunny's mind whirled as he faked rabbit punches at his comatose opponent. If the Marvel lost in North Bay, they'd probably both be fired. The only way for the Marvel to win was if Bunny got disqualified.

Just then the referee bent over them, completely puzzled at the sudden shift of plot. But when the crowd began hooting in derision, he had no other recourse than to start his count.

Which is when the brainy Bunny leaped to his feet, muttered "Sorry pal," and then – letting loose the first unfaked uppercut of his entire wrestling career – knocked the ref out cold.

Although the famed Dodger slugger **Babe Herman** could hammer a ball into orbit, he was notoriously lacking in fielding. One day, he received a frantic call from a bank official informing him that some imposter had signed Herman's name to worthless checks and cashed three of them that week.

Herman gave it a second's thought, then suggested, "Tell ya what. The next time the guy comes in, take him out to the parking lot and lob a few flies at him."

"And *what*, sniffed the banker, "is *that* supposed to prove?"

"Well," said Babe, "if he *catches* any, you'll know it ain't me."

In his bout with **Sugar Ray Leonard,** Argentine boxer **Daniel Gonzales** was kayoed in the first round. Minutes later, in the dressing room, he was asked if Leonard was the best man he'd ever fought.

"I dunno," mumbled Gonzales. "I wasn't in there long enough to find out."

After being knocked out by **Tami Mauiello**, boxer **Bruce Woodcock** was asked which punch had bothered him the most.

"Jesus," snapped Woodcock, "the *last* one, a'course."

After reading a story about the previous day's game in the *Milwaukee Journal*, the Braves shortstop **Johnny Logan** called the paper to complain that they'd made a mistake.

The following day the paper ran a correction, claiming the mistake had been a typographical error.

"The hell it was," Logan snorted. "It was a clean base hit."

During his peak, **Rogie Vachon** was the L.A. Kings' main goalie. His backup, **Gary Simmons**, spent most games on the bench. But after Vachon had played 20 straight games, Simmons was finally put in. After he won the game, the press crowded around. One reporter asked when his next start would be.

"What the hell do you think I *am?*" snarled Simmons. "A *MACHINE?*"

Ballplayer **Stan Roberts** was a gargantuan man, and **Pat Williams** never let him forget it. Every time he talked to a writer, Williams zapped his buddy with a sizzling new "fat" barb. For instance:

"You know the old saying, 'No man is an island.' Well Stanley comes close."

"Stanley's chosen his burial site: the State of Montana."

"We got him eating the seven basic food groups, and now there are only two left."

"The other night, we had to remove an obstruction from Stanley's throat. It was a pizza."

Still, when Roberts' weight plunged below 300 pounds, Williams had to soften his barbs. "I can't use those fat jokes any more," he lamented. "Stanley's turned over a new chin."

But when Roberts at last slimmed down to fighting form, Williams reluctantly fired his final salvo. "Both McDonald's and Wendy's are suing him for non-support."

A hulking Notre Dame tackle constantly bored his teammates by bragging about his strength. One day, his coach snapped. "Awright, muscles," he said calmly, "I'll bet ya fifty bucks I could push a load in a wheel barrow that *you* couldn't even budge."

"Hah!" sneered the tackle, "you're on."

When a barrow was wheeled up, the coach eyed the bulging brute. "Okay big-mouth," he barked. "Get *in*."

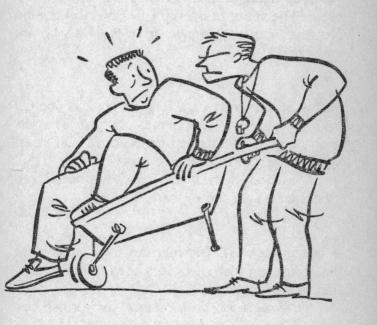

Casey Stengel once summed it all up in a sentence: "The secret of managing a club is to keep the five guys who hate ya away from the five who are undecided."

One Sunday morning, a surgeon got a phone call from a colleague inviting him to play golf. The surgeon hung up and dashed to the door. "Oh, dear," said his wife, "not another emergency."

"Afraid so," he said. "And it sounds serious. Three other doctors are already there."

Fight manager **Al Braverman** took umbrage at the accusation that his boxers used a foreign substance on their gloves.

"It is *not* a foreign substance," Braverman bellowed. "Dammit, it's made right here in the U.S.A."

When umpire **Jocko Conlan** once called a strike on the Phillies' **Richie Ashburn**, Richie turned around and screamed, "*WHAT?*"

Jocko glowered back for a minute, then snarled, "Okay then, *you* umpire. Call the next damn pitch yourself.

Ashburn was so stunned he never moved his bat as the next one smacked the catcher's mitt. Peeking back over his shoulder, Ashburn asked, "Strike?"

"Richie," boomed Jocko, "in the history of baseball, you just had the only chance to both bat and umpire. And you bloody well blew it!"

Over the decades, hockey fans have heaved everything onto the ice: eggs, live chickens, squealing pigs, squids. For example, The Montreal Forum was once famous for its toe rubbers. Every time some hometown star like Boom Boom or the Rocket scored a goal, the rink would be littered with the winter footwear.

Before one game in the Forum, Chicago Black Hawk **Dennis Hull** was beckoned aside by his brother. Expecting some tip from the golden one, Dennis joined him in a corner.

"Dennis," murmured **Bobby Hull**, "when the Habs score tonight and the rubbers hit the ice, grab me a good pair of size tens, willya?"

After Los Angeles Laker **Hot Rod Hundley** turned sportscaster, he was asked about his fondest memory in basketball. "Well," he said, "my biggest thrill was definitely the night **Elgin Baylor** and I combined for 73 points in Madison Square Garden.

"Mind you, Elgin had 71 of them."

What was **Bob Hope's** opinion about the former U.S. president **Gerald Ford's** athletic abilities? "We have 51 golf courses in Palm Springs," Bob noted. "Ford never decides which one he'll play till after his first tee shot."

Sports broadcaster **Don Cherry** had a female English bull terrier named Blue that he adored. But after the little bitch bit Cherry's wife, Rose, a friend finally told him, "Listen, you're gonna have to get rid of her."

"I know," Cherry said sadly. "Me and Blue will really miss her."

Few athletes are averse to boasting. But the Boston Celtics' **Larry Bird** might have out-bragged them all. Asked to address his teammates at a celebration of their 1981 NBA championship, Larry took the mike and purred, "I could stand up here all night praising the whole team. But I'm getting tired of talking only about me."

During his tenure with the St. Louis Blues, **George Morrison** wasn't coach **Scotty Bowman's** best-loved player. After sitting on the bench for two straight games, Morrison was warming it again when, late in a match against Los Angeles, he suddenly got ravenous. After bribing an usher to sneak him a hot dog, George was taking his first bite when Bowman barked, "Morrison, get in there and kill that penalty."

Totally rattled, Morrison shoved the hot dog in his glove as he scampered over the boards. And sure enough, in a scrimmage in front of his net seconds later, an opposing player slammed him.

The weenie shot from his mitt like a missile before spiraling to the ice. George's goalie – thinking it a puck – dropped to block it. Just then the whistle blew.

Yanking his star gourmet from the game, Bowman shrieked, "Dammit, if ya hafta eat, do it on your own time."

During a game between the Leafs and Red Wings, the formidable **King Clancy** was refereeing. But the Toronto team was convinced that Clancy was out to nail them that night since he'd been giving them far more infractions than Detroit.

At one point — while two Leafs sat huddled in the penalty box, and all the Red Wings were on the ice — Leaf defenceman **Babe Pratt** accidentally backed into Clancy, flipping him onto his fanny.

King was furious. "You son of a bitch," he snarled. "I wish I was playing against you tonight."

"Well," frowned Pratt, pointing at the penalty box, "*aren't* you?"

California's Hillcrest Country Club has a rule that players must wear trousers at all times. It's all because one sweltering day, two members, **Harpo Marx** and **George Burns**, took off their shirts. But after four holes, the irate manager chugged out to tell them that going shirtless was against the rules.

So the two players went into a huddle, and instantly pulled off their pants.

One night, hours after curfew, Montreal Canadiens' star **Peter Mahovlich** reeled into his hotel lobby to be confronted by his fuming coach, **Scotty Bowman.**

"Awright, wiseguy," snarled Scotty, "that'll cost you a hundred bucks."

"Y'got it, chief," nodded Mahovlich, and slowly peeled off $200.

Bowman was confused. "What the hell's the extra hundred for?"

"Ah, *you* know," Mahovlich shrugged. "The next time I get caught."

After his Buccaneers lost a major game, a reporter asked Tampa Bay football coach **John McKay** what he thought of his team's execution.

McKay pondered a second, then snarled, "I think it's a good idea."

Detroit Lions' linesman **Alex Karras** was once suspended for betting on games — but apparently learned his lesson. When, a few months later, he was asked by an official to call a coin flip at midfield, Karras was aghast.

"Dammit," he snarled. "You *know* I'm not allowed to gamble."

On the first tee of Michigan's Red Run Golf Club, the same **Alex Karras** smacked his ball through the huge plate glass window of the clubhouse bar. Trotting over to the building, Karras poked his head through the shattered window.

"Hey guys," he asked the startled patrons, "is this room out of bounds?"

Ballplayer **Bob Brenly** was aghast at this pal, **Kevin Mitchell's**, outlandish fur coats. "He's the only guy I know who shops at the San Diego Zoo," Bob snorted. "With just one outfit, five animals suddenly hit the endangered species list."

University of Texas basketball coach **Abe Lemons** was asked if his team should be ranked in the Top 20. Abe took ages to consider the question. Finally, he said, "You mean in the State?"

Lemons told reporters that the two guys who'd just stormed out of his office were disgruntled alumni. "They wanted to buy up my contract," Abe explained. "But neither had change for a twenty."

After the Toronto Maple Leaf's demon scorer **Darryl Sittler** slapped six shots into the Boston net one game, he said he felt sorry for the goalie. "I hear the poor guy was so depressed," Sittler smiled, "that he went and stood on a railway track — and the train shot between his legs."

Because Greta was by far the best golfer in the Vancouver club, her hubby Arnie, basking in reflected glory, always caddied.

Approaching the 18th hole one afternoon, Greta checked her scorecard and suddenly realized she could shatter the club record if she made the par three.

But alas, the ball sliced — and landed in a field behind a farmer's barn. Greta was shattered until the faithful Arnie checked its location and yelped, "Lookit here! This barn's got big doors on both sides. If you pitch through them to the green, you can *still* make par. Just be *sure* you don't hit the rafters."

So he opened both doors, and Greta took her

shot. But the ball smacked the rafters, rebounded like a bullet onto Arnie's head, and dropped him dead.

Three years went by. Greta remarried and was back on the course one afternoon with her new hubby, Harry, who was caddying. But precisely the same thing happened on the 18th hole. When Greta whacked the ball behind the barn, Harry proudly noted that it had two doors. "You can *still* make par if you pitch straight through them," he pointed out. "But you won't have a chance if you hit the rafters."

"You're telling *me*!" Greta snapped. "I was in this exact situation three years ago. And it took me five strokes to get onto the green."

In the 1973 Stanley Cup playoffs, Bruins center **Phil Esposito** was front-ended by Ranger **Ron Harris**. Rushed to a Boston hospital, Phil's leg was encased in a cast.

But the day of their post-season bash, the Bruins decided their NHL scoring champ had to be there. So sneaking into Esposito's room, they stealthily wheeled Phil's bed to a service elevator and out a back exit.

Then, to a chorus of car horns as they whipped Phil's bed down a boulevard, the team thundered up to an intersection. "Signal a left, Espo," shouted Bobby Orr.

And obediently, Phil shot his arm out.

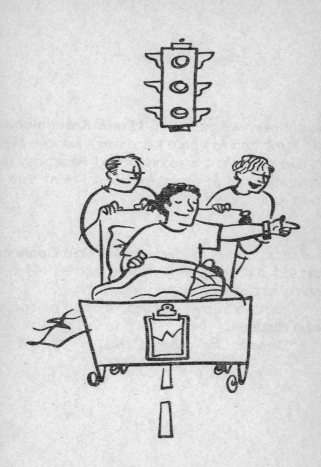

Light-heavyweight champ **Maxie Rosenbloom** said some gamblers once made him a lucrative offer to take a dive in the second round. Reluctantly, he admitted, "I had to turn them down. I didn't think I could go the distance."

Oakland Raiders middle linebacker **Dan Conners** was such a rotten golfer that after shooting 144 in a tournament, he won the booby prize.

"You should have cheated," snorted his coach, **John Madden.**

"Dammit," Dan muttered, "I *did.*"

Jocks get their name for the straps they wear – but sometimes even that equipment fails to protect. One night, **Doug Barkley** got a speeding puck in the groin, and collapsed to the ice in agony.

Gordie Howe instantly skated to his stricken teammate and, to assure him his testicles were still intact, bent over and said, "Doug, open your mouth."

Though Barkley in his pain had no clue what Howe meant, he obediently opened his jaw. Gordie peered in, then instantly beamed. "Aha," he shouted triumphantly. "*THERE* they are!"

Most athletes learn to bear the verbal slings of irate fans silently. But not major leaguer **Danny Murtaugh.**

Whenever the infielder played Chicago, one front row fan heckled him incessantly. But, on one especially vociferous day, Danny had endured enough.

Dashing to the stands, he grabbed his nemesis by the shirt. "Listen loudmouth," Danny snarled, "when I was a kid on the farm we had a stupid, stubborn jackass. One evening I gave it such a thrashing, my daddy heard it braying, and then beat *me*.

"'Someday,' he warned me, 'that jackass is gonna haunt you.'"

"And ya know," Murtaugh glowered, "until now, I never believed him."

Murtaugh swore this story was true. He said that during spring training, he and roommate **Ernie White** spent one entire night on the town, heading straight for the ballpark in the morning. Both of them looked like sacks of sawdust.

Their manager spied them and ambled over. "You boys have a good night's sleep?" he smiled.

"Sure did, Skip," beamed Danny.

"Well, I'm glad to hear that," the manager said. "I was worried ya mighta been a bit disturbed."

"Disturbed? Danny frowned. "By *what*, Skip."

"By the tractor-trailer," the manager roared, "that crashed through your hotel room at 4 a.m."

Brooklyn Dodgers' shortstop **Bobby Morgan** was so irate when a ball bounced through his legs that he muttered to center fielder **Duke Snyder**, "Dammit! I swear that's the last error I'll make this year."

Two innings later, when a similar ball shot between Morgan's legs, Snyder shouted over, "Happy New Year, Bobby."

After another Brooklyn Dodgers' shortstop, **Bill Russell**, had five errors in a double header, his pal Mel Durslag snorted, "I've seen better hands on a clock."

While sports stars are famous for going A.W.O.L., it ain't only after curfew.

Victoria Cougars' goalie **Hec Fowler** was such a crazed fire buff that at least two opening playoffs were delayed – because, on his way to the games, Hec roared off after passing fire trucks. (Then, he stayed at the blazes to direct operations.)

Some hockey players disappear even during games. After one obstreperous fan had driven him batty, **Jean Baptiste Pusie** dove over the boards and tore after him.

When the guy dashed outside, Pusie (still in skates) pursued – clattering behind him for two blocks. But so obviously hopeless was the chase that Pusie finally puffed up outside a bar, and stopped.

Then, clomping in with stick still gripped, he plopped on a stool and snarled, "Oh hell, gimme a beer."

Yet hockey's greatest disappearing act took place within inches of the Montreal Forum's ice. During a game with the Canadiens, the Maple Leafs' **Ted Kennedy** skated into the face-off circle and glanced at his right-winger, who was there. Then he glanced toward his left-winger, **Bob Davidson,** who — though he'd been there a second ago — *wasn't* any longer.

It seems that while Kennedy was peering around, two Montreal fans had jerked Bob across the boards, and were punching him out in the aisle.

The Chicago Cubs' manager **Charlie Grimm** got a frantic phone call from a scout in a tiny Arkansas town. "Hey, Boss," jabbered the scout, "I've just seen the world's most amazing pitcher — and the kid's right here beside me. This afternoon, he pitched a no-hitter."

"Yeah?" said Grimm.

"Yeah," the scout shouted. "But you've never seen a no-hitter *like* it. He fired 27 strikeouts in a row. No one even brushed the ball."

"*No* one?" asked Grimm.

"Well, yeah," said the scout, "until the last winning when some guy popped a foul. So whaddaya say? Shall I sign him up?"

"Hell no," snorted Grimm. "Sign the guy who got the foul. We need *hitters*."

A golfer swacked his ball across a high knoll on the fairway. After trudging over the top, he saw a man spread-eagled on the ground. Rushing down, he pulled the guy to a sitting position and stammered, "I'm terribly sorry. Are you badly hurt?"

"Yes, I am," said the guy, wobbling to his feet. "I'm also a lawyer. And I'm going to sue you for five thousand bucks."

"But," gasped the golfer, "I did yell 'fore.'"

"Alright," said the lawyer. "I'll take it."

After an embarrassing hockey game, player **Phil Watson** faced the press in the locker room.

"Gentlemen," he announced, "I have absolutely nothing to say. Any questions?"

Before world lightweight champ **Benny Leonard** won his title, which he held for eight years, he'd lost a couple of fights. One was to a boxer six inches shorter.

Later, a fan asked, "How could ya ever let that guy beat ya, Benny? He only came up to your chin."

"Yeah," said Leonard. "But he came up to it too often."

Considering himself a clothes horse, coach **Chuck Daly** didn't mind paying for fancy threads. But he balked the day a salesman tried to sell him a suit for twelve hundred bucks.

"You gotta be **kidding**," Daly yelped. "What makes it so expensive?"

"But sir," purred the clerk, "this suit's made entirely from virgin wool."

"Well, hell," said Daly, "if that's how you price 'em, show me something from a sheep that's fooled around a little."

Los Angeles Dodgers' manager **Tommy Lasorda** was reputed to be a tightwad. But when Dodger pitcher **Don Sutton** was asked to confirm it, he growled, "That's not fair. Every year, Tommy offers $50,000 to the family of the unknown soldier."

Baseball manager **Branch Rickey** was infamous for his stinginess. During a reunion of the St. Louis Cardinals' Gashouse Gang, Rickey praised the squad as "men who loved the game so much they would have played for nothing."

To which player **Pepper Martin** piped up: "Yeah, and thanks to you, we almost did."

After living to 83, **Rickey** once mused about the stages of senility. "First you forget names," Branch said. "Then you forget faces. Then you forget to zip up your fly. And then you forget to unzip your fly."

Funny lines about skiing are thankfully few. But humorist **Erma Bombeck** probably fired off the best one. "I do not," she stated, "participate in *any* sport with ambulances at the bottom of the hill."

There aren't many jokes about jogging either. **Milton Berle** said his doctor told him it could add years to his life. "And I think he was right," agreed Berle. "I feel ten years older already."

While Texas basketball coach **Abe Lemons** swore he'd never jog because, "If I die, I want to be sick."

It was one of those days. The New York Yankees had suffered a disastrous 9 to 0 defeat. Afterwards in the locker room, **Billy Martin** glowered at his players. "When I get through managing," he growled, "I'm going to open a kindergarten.

"At the moment, I'll have to settle for a vein."

Green Bay Packers' coach **Vince Lombardi** was famous for instilling fear in his players. As tight-end **Max McGee** put it, "When Vince shouts 'Siddown,' I don't even look for a chair."

But Packer **Henry Jordan** conceded, "At least he's *fair*. He treats us all the same – like dogs."

The "Big Train", **Walter Johnson**, may have been the fastest pitcher ever. He was, in fact, so swift that once, in the gathering dusk of a final inning, catcher **Eddie Ainsmith** suggested he just *pretend* to pitch the ball. Walter grinningly agreed. So after his right arm flashed forward, Ainsmith whacked his mitt, and the umpire shouted, "Strike!"

"You blind buzzard," screamed the batter. "That goddam ball was a *foot* outside."

Two-Ton Tony Galento looked more like a beachball than a boxer, and most sportswriters considered his heavyweight title fight with **Joe Louis** a complete mismatch. Still, Tony stunned them all when, early in the bout, he dropped Louis to the canvas with a fast left hook.

Surprised but unscathed, Joe sprang to his feet before the ref even started to count. At the end of the round, his trainer, **Jack Blackburn,** gave the champ hell. "I've told you a dozen times to take the count when that happens. Why didn't you stay down for nine?"

"What?" said Joe. "And let Tony get all that rest?"

Before a playoff game in the 1930's, Chicago Cub pitcher **Guy Bush** told trainer **Andy Lotshaw** he had a sore arm.

Andy considered the problem to be more in Bush's brain than his bicep. But, to placate the player, he said he had a fabulous cure. So pouring dark liquid from a bottle, he lavished it all over Guy's arm.

After Bush won with no further pain, he insisted on a rubdown with the miracle potion before each successive game. And, because Guy's arm had stopped aching, Lotshaw willingly obliged.

Yet even when Guy was finally traded, his trainer never told him the truth: he'd been swabbing him down for all those years with Coca-Cola.

Although the New York Yankees were known for sartorial splendor, their star catcher **Yogi Berra** always went on the road with a valise resembling a Boer War relic. Finally, a disgusted manager snorted, "Hey Berra, why don't you spend a few bucks and buy yourself a new suitcase?"

"What *for?*" argued Yogi. "I only use it when I travel."

A bellboy carried **Berra's** valise into a hotel room. Yogi scanned the room and asked, "Where's the bed?"

"Oh," smiled the bellboy, "it's a Murphy bed. It's standing up behind that door in the wall."

"Well, get me another room," scowled Yogi. "I ain't gonna sleep nowhere standing up."

The brainy Yankees' ballplayer **Bobby Brown** spent a rainy day in the dugout reading the weighty tome, "Gray's Anatomy." When he finally closed the cover, **Yogi Berra**, who'd been sitting beside him, set down his comic book and asked, "Well, how did *yours* turn out?"

After a celebrated career in the majors, **Berra** was interviewed back in hometown St. Louis by his old friend, **Jack Buck**, host of a local radio show. After the broadcast, Buck handed him a check which read, "Pay to Bearer."

"Ahh, Jack," Yogi said sadly, "you've known me for years, and still can't spell my name right."

Berra made it into baseball's Hall of Fame. But he is better remembered today for his unique observations on life — like the time when he was watching TV and an old Steve McQueen movie came on. "Oh," said Yogi, "he must of made that before he died."

Or when a bunch of his teammates kept bugging him to go see a dirty movie. After numerous refusals, Yogi finally gave in. "Okay," he said. "Who's in it?"

Or when a waitress asked him if he wanted his pizza cut into eight slices or four, Yogi said, "Four. I don't think I can eat eight."

Or, at a humid New York gala, when Mayor Lindsay's wife said, "You look nice and cool, Yogi," and he smiled back: "Thanks, you don't look so hot yourself."

Or once, when the Berras were redecorating, his son called upstairs, "Dad, the man is here for the Venetian blinds." "Look in my wallet," Yogi shouted down, "and give them a five buck donation."

Or when a friend drove by with a dog in the back of his car and asked, "What do you think of my daughter's Afghan?" "Looks nice," nodded Yogi, "but I'm thinking of getting a Chevy Vega."

Yet Yogi says he *never* called those low-slung German dogs "Datsuns." Nor, he swears, did he advise a rookie: "Always go to other people's funerals or they won't come to yours."

But then, Berra admits, "I really didn't say *everything* I said."

During a game against Los Angeles, Minnesota defenceman **Mike McMahon** made an appalling pass, allowing the Kings to score. After the first period, North Stars coach **Wren Blair** stormed into the dressing room, whipped off his jacket, and threw it at McMahon. During his outburst, Blair slipped on an orange peel and fell flat on the floor. He was lying there still shouting when his trainer walked in.

The following day on an airplane, his trainer gave him a nudge: "Hey Wren, tell me something," he murmured confidentially. "When you were spread-eagled out on the floor last night, what the hell kind of play were you trying to demonstrate?"

Stopping by the paddock at Toronto's Woodbine racetrack, the notorious horseplayer **Freddie Ross** noticed a priest bless a nag named Brigadoon. But Ross thought nothing more about it – until Brigadoon breezed first across the finish line.

Dashing back to the paddock, Freddie saw the priest bless another long shot named Midnight. Even though Midnight was listed at 25 to 1, Freddie placed fifty bucks to win. And indeed, Midnight did – hitting the finish line by half a length. And so it went all afternoon. All of the priest's horses won.

Freddie knew he should quit when he was ahead. But after all, the good father had picked every winner. So, on the final race, Freddie bet his entire wad on Patty's Promise, a 30 to 1 shot that he'd seen the priest visit.

The horse came out like a catapult, but soon lost steam and finished last. Freddie was livid. "What happened in the last race?" he roared at the father. "That blasted nag shoulda been dogfood."

"Ah," sighed the priest, "that's the problem with you Protestants. You can't tell the difference between blessings and last rites."

Racetrack addict **Henny Youngman** may well have wagered on the same race himself. "I bet on a horse at ten to one," he said. "It didn't come in until half-past five."

After the Philadelphia Phillies blew a 15-game lead, their manager **Danny Ozark** grumped, "Well hell, even Napoleon had his Watergate."

When a writer asked the Los Angeles Lakers guard **Gail Goodrich** what the team does after 10 a.m. practices, Gail giggled, "Hey, ya gotta be kidding. We go back to the hotel and wake up Wilt."

The catcher **Choo Choo Coleman** was one of the friendliest New York Mets — if not the most astute. But he couldn't remember anyone's name if they had it tattooed on their chin.

Charlie Neal, after rooming with Choo Choo for an entire season, saw him again at spring training. "I'm going to go over and say hi to Choo Choo," Neal told the other players, "but I'll betcha he doesn't know my name."

"C'mon," said one teammate, "that's ridiculous." But they followed Neal as he crossed the field and stuck out his hand. "Hey Choo, good to see you."

Coleman gave him an enormous grin. "Well, *hi* there," he replied.

"Do you know who I am?" Neal asked.

"Of *course*," beamed Choo Choo. "You're number four."

Kansas City Royals' sportscaster **Fred White** read a wire-service clip that mistakenly showed the same starter and relief pitcher for the Minnesota Twins. Turning back to his microphone, Fred chirped, "Well folks, I see in the second inning of the game in Minnesota that Terry Felton has relieved himself on the mound."

A New York Rangers' defenceman, who'll remain anonymous, was in the Stanley Cup finals when the game ended 1-1 in regulation time.

But then, during overtime, a Canadien player slapped a shot between his skates — scoring the winning goal.

Afterwards, in the dressing room's stony silence, the player slinked over to his coach. "Hey sorry, coach," he murmured, "I shoulda kept my legs together."

"I just wish your mother had," snarled the coach.

A grizzled old maritimer took a beginner out fishing in his rowboat. After twenty minutes, the novice turned and said, "Say, do you have any more of those plastic floats?"

"What's wrong with the one I gave you?" the old man grumped.

"I dunno," the youngster shrugged. "But every few minutes it keeps sinking."

Asked if his marriage to **Marilyn Monroe** had been good for him, **Joe DiMaggio** snapped, "It was better than rooming with Joe Page."

After playing 18 holes on a wicked, sleet-swept day, two craggy Scots sat shivering by the fire. As the ice slowly melted from their beards, the wind outside screamed in from the sea and hailstones rattled the windows. After silently sipping Scotch for an hour, Mac finally rose to his feet. "Well Rob, I'm off. Tomorrow then? Same time?"

"Aye," nodded Rob. "Weather permittin'."

The great slugger **Hank Aaron** once bragged to his teammates in a bar: "It took me 17 years, but I finally got 3,000 hits. It happened yesterday on the golf course."

Atlanta Hawks' forward **John Drew** also had a problem with official questions. When called to the front office to provide information for an insurance form, a secretary asked him his date of birth. "September 30th," Drew snapped back.

But when she asked, "What year?" Drew looked puzzled.

"In what *year?*" she repeated, "is your birthdate?"

Suddenly aware of the trick question, Drew beamed. "Ah! *Every* year. *Right?*"

It was Chicago defenceman **Tom Reid's** first NHL game. The 19-year-old was on the ice for only seconds when, clearing the puck from his end zone, he was slammed – "as hard," he said, "as I've ever been hit" – by Detroit Red Wing great **Gordie Howe.**

He hit the ice unconscious. When he tried to get up, he collapsed again. His eyes were blurred, his knees spaghetti. When he finally staggered to the bench, coach **Billy Reay** growled, "What the hell you doing back here, Reid?"

"Coach," Tom choked, "I think that old guy just blinded me. I can't *see* outta my right eye."

"No wonder," snapped Reay. "Your bloody helmet's on sideways."

The New York Yankees' **Don Larsen** was asked if he ever got tired of talking about the perfect game he pitched in the 1956 World Series.

"No," frowned Don. "Why should I?"

The night he was inducted into the Hall of Fame, **Dizzy Dean** strode to the dais, acknowledged the thunderous cheers, and said humbly, "Well, now I guess I'm amongst them mortals."

Football's **Bronko Nagurski** fell into the same league as baseball's Berra, Stengel, and Dean when it came to ludicrous lines. Once, after scuffling with a teammate in a hotel room and tumbling through a second-storey window, Nagurski lay surrounded by a crowd on a sidewalk.

He'd just staggered to his feet when a cop dashed up and snarled, "What the hell's going on here?"

"I've no idea," mumbled Bronko. "I just got here myself."

And, with special thanks to those athletes, reporters, announcers and fans — who shared with us their favorite sports fiascos or slapshot punchlines. They include: Tom Alderman, Del Andison, Brian Budd, Glen Becker, Joe Bowen, Oscar Brooks, David Cobb, Peggy Dean, Ron Ellis, Gerry Hall, Al Dickie, E. Kaye Fulton, Howard King, Ken Lusk, John MacDonald,

Tom MacMillan, Colin McDonald, Bob & Liz Martyn, Nelson Millman, Ron McLean, Bob Oakes, Jim Proudfoot, Bob Purcell, John & Mary Richmond, Jack Robinson, Fred Ross, David Scott, Mitch Smyth, Doug Speer, Al Sokol, Brian Vallee, and especially — the week before retiring his typewriter — that grand old gladiator of the Toronto Star's sports pages, Milt Dunnell.